T0198401

This Is Us

"We were poor but we had love"

Republic, Missouri

1951

Copyright © 2023 Linda P. Long.

All rights reserved. No part of this book may be used or reproduced by any means, graphic, electronic, or mechanical, including photocopying, recording, taping or by any information storage retrieval system without the written permission of the author except in the case of brief quotations embodied in critical articles and reviews.

This book is a work of non-fiction. Unless otherwise noted, the author and the publisher make no explicit guarantees as to the accuracy of the information contained in this book and in some cases, names of people and places have been altered to protect their privacy.

Archway Publishing books may be ordered through booksellers or by contacting:

Archway Publishing
1663 Liberty Drive
Bloomington, IN 47403
www.archwaypublishing.com
844-669-3957

Because of the dynamic nature of the Internet, any web addresses or links contained in this book may have changed since publication and may no longer be valid. The views expressed in this work are solely those of the author and do not necessarily reflect the views of the publisher, and the publisher hereby disclaims any responsibility for them.

Interior Image Credit: Barbie Williams

ISBN: 978-1-6657-4628-1 (sc)
978-1-6657-4627-4 (hc)
978-1-6657-4629-8 (e)

Library of Congress Control Number: 2023911644

Print information available on the last page.

Archway Publishing rev. date: 06/28/2023

This Is Us

"We were poor but we had love"

By Linda P. Long

Illustrated by Barbie Williams
Designed & edited by Charlie Johnson

In Memory of

Marvin L. Long

I dedicate this book to my children:

Lisa Hays

Gregory Johnson

Sheila Powell

Charlie Johnson

Richard Long

Christina Cunningham

This is a story about a poor family
who lives in a small town during the 1950s.

TABLE OF CONTENTS

CHAPTER 1

Two Poor Girls

Two little, poor girls live each day as an adventure. The fourteen months difference in their ages was not a big deal to either of us. Glenda was the brains of the two--its first Naomi was shy, and Glenda was anything but shy. Glenda woke each day with some wheels turning. What could she do today? Glenda, the child who never talked until two years old. Her mom had an old radio on a table by her iron baby bed. So, her first words were the jingle to the advertisement for Tide detergent.

We had concrete floors, so my glass baby bottles were brought every night after the milk was gone. I crashed them on the floor then I got older and went out on a pile of lumber, naked at three, and yelled: "Hi! Ho! Silver!"

We lived close to the sidewalk, and I would pick up cigarette butts and smoke them behind our old upright piano. It didn't matter who threw them down; at three one doesn't care where their fix comes from. My mother would catch me every time. She said the smoke would come rolling up from the back. I was little and could get behind there.

So, we played with tin cans, coffee cans were the short kind. They were our bowls. We made things like grass salad and chocolate gravy—one of our favorites that mom made us. It's just hot pudding.

We walked to school in snow. Our mother ordered striped socks, boys' socks, because she said they would match all our dress colors. Well, we took them off as soon as we got to the church just up from our house. But next fall, she got more. She said they lasted so well and never faded. I think she really wanted two boys. She dressed us in boys' shirts and jeans.

CHAPTER 2

Hero Township

I come from Republic, Missouri. It was a small, rural town back in the 1950s. It had one street that ran through downtown, a laundry mat, a bank, a café, one drug store, a hardware store, a Western Auto, a MFA, three general stores, a beauty shop, a barber shop, and a post office.

Saturdays were busy days in the small town. We had a town drunk who always got in the drunk tank on weekends. It was a small jail behind the hardware store. My sister Naomi and I felt sorry for him. We got money from him and took him cokes. We had a sheriff who had a spotlight on his car covered with red cellophane paper and wire. He turned it on and moved it back and forth to look like a real cop car light blinking. Yep, he was a Barney Fife, but we never had trouble.

We were poor back then and had no plumbing. It was an all- American town. At Christmas time the city decorated the lamp posts on Main Street with beautiful angels, stockings, Santa bells and stars. All the small shops and stores decorated their windows beautifully. It was wonderful for us poor kids and we loved it.

CHAPTER 3

Summertime

We didn't care in the summer when school was out. I was the brains of the little group. We had two sisters and one girl my age. Two cousins who were always living off our family and one lived with us. Really, I was the instigator of the group. We did things like go to the dump for pop bottles to sell at the grocery store for a nickel each. Afterwards, we were off to the candy store. A dime each is what we shared. It got us a bag full of candy.

We would go to the old band stand and sit on the stage and sing or just eat candy. Every day, I came up with Naomi and me ways to get money. One day we went to old lady Whipper's to pull weeds out of her garden. It was a dirty hot job. She gave us fifty cents each. For many hours she would come out to see if we got every weed. Naomi didn't like this idea. As soon as we got our money, we washed up at home in the faucet and ran to the dime store to get Judy, our baby sister, a toy. We were crazy over our little sister. She was so happy when we got her little tea sets or all kinds of cheap toys. I remember a top that you pushed the handle down. It went fast and hummed. She loved it.

In summer, Mom got a tub of water and Life Boy soap. She and Aunt Hazel scrubbed us kids till we were almost raw. My cousins Donna and Johnnie were there a lot in summer. Aunt Hazel could drive. She took us to the orchard a lot to pick grapes, apples, and peaches. They sat out under our old tree beside our house and ate the pickings. After they finished it was time to scrub ears. Aunt Hazel would scrub Johnnie's ears so hard they were red.

She said: "Get over here. Them rusty things."

He would just frown and cry: "Wait, wait…" and she got them clean.

Our little gang ran all over town. One day, Naomi and I went behind a store that was moving. I was going through some boxes.

Naomi said: "Leave them."

I opened a little box and there was a five-dollar bill inside! We ran fast to our house to show Mom.

She said: "Give it to me. When I go to Salvation Army on

Saturday I will get you some clothes."

I told Naomi outside we should have just blown it. Naomi agreed but we knew it was best to let Mom have it.

CHAPTER 4

Mrs. Roper

So, I said: "Let's get the gang and go to the dump."

When you're poor, you first go on to the next thing to get some cash like dirty pop bottles. My mind was always thinking of ways to get cash.

I told Naomi: "Let's go to Mrs. Roper's."

She was an old lady who just lay in bed all day. She was tall, but we never saw her standing. She was as long as the twin bed and even longer because her feet hung over the end of the bed. Her feet were long and thin. I thought she looked funny because her hair was real long, and she had no teeth.

I was a silly little girl. I would get her to sing "Abide with Me." We would look at each other and grin. At first, we thought she was a witch, but we thought she looked like a witch, but she sung about the Lord.

We got to her house and asked: "Mrs. Roper, can we wash your dishes?"

She said yes. She had a lot. We did them and she gave us a whole dollar. We went to town and got candy and something for our baby sister.

Wow. We were smart. We didn't go to Mom first. We spent the money instead. We kept doing dishes. Then one day, she asked us to do her laundry. We took it to the laundry house. She gave us money for the washer and dryer and laundry soap. We saw her gowns had poop on them, so we didn't touch them. We threw them in and poured a lot of soap on them. They came clean and we dried and folded them. We took them to her, and she gave us five dollars!

We went to town and bought Mom a beautiful cut glass bowl, a doll for Judy, and the rest we spent on candy for us. Mom always asked where we got our money, and we told her.

The next day, Edith, an old fat lady who was mentally challenged came to our house. She told Mom she was going to kill us because we took her job! She was doing laundry for Mrs. Roper. Mrs. Roper told her us girls got them clean. Edith was washing them out by hand and keeping all the money.

Mom ran her off.

Edith came back a few days later. Mom told her to quit talking so loudly because we girls were taking a nap. I was on a pallet on the floor. I kept tossing and turning.

Mom said: "Glenda, go to sleep."

I said: "Tell Edith to put her legs together." I was tired of looking at that thing. Edith got mad and left.

CHAPTER 5

Glenda...
Always Getting in Trouble

When I was only four, Naomi used to laugh at me. Mom put butter on my lips to keep the flies off and that made them worse. I don't know where she got the idea that butter would keep them off. My lips, I guess, were like ice on a road—maybe she thought they would slide off.

I was always getting into trouble. Aunt Hazel came running in one day.

She told Mom: "Tell that jewelry salesman that I'm not here."

She hid in a closet next to our front door. There was no door, just a piece of material covering it. Mom made a long curtain to cover it. The man came up to the front door. He knocked and Mom went to it.

He came inside and asked: "Is Mrs. Hazel Coker here?" Mom said: "I haven't seen her."

I was standing there and spoke up: "She is right here" and pulled back the curtain.

She gave him some money and he left.

Aunt Hazel laughed and said: "You little stinker." Mom said: "You made a liar out of me."

She told Daddy at supper. He laughed so hard.

Mom said: "I will not do that again. I will first tell

Hazel…no, Glenda will tell on me."

One day, we were all outside. We heard some weird music. We all peeked into the front room window. Mom had an axe! She was chopping up the old upright piano. Since I smoked behind it, she cut it up, carried it out, and burned it.

She looked at me and said: "Now you will not be smoking behind that thing anymore."

She was a strong old woman.

CHAPTER 6

My Brothers Ronnie and John

Our older brother, Ronnie, was always playing tricks on us. He got on top of the smoke house and told us to jump. We sailed down. Our little dresses were like parachutes and we floated down slowly. Then he jumped and landed in some old bed springs and sprang his ankle. He chased us to the house. When Mom and Dad came home, his ankle was swollen big.

The fair was going on in town so Dad said he could still take us little girls.

He said: "Dad, my ankle."

Dad said: "No, you said you would take them, and you are going to."

He hobbled behind us telling us what he was going to do to us when his ankle got well. He said he was going to make us smell his dirty socks. He wore Converse high tops, and his socks would stand up—they were bad.

Ronnie always fell asleep in church. Mom always took us to church. We walked two blocks to church. We would start home from church and Mom would say: "Get Ronnie." So, we always went to the back seat and there he was sound asleep. We would get him up. He stumbled around us little girls. We each took ahold of his hands, one on each side, while he sleepwalked. So, we led him in mud puddles, down in muddy ditches, if there was snow, through big snow drifts. We would get him home and get him ready for bed. He would always wonder how he got home and how he got so wet. We would snicker and go to bed.

One time, Ronnie mixed up everything in the refrigerator. Mustard, mayo, milk, catsup, and pickle juice…whatever he could think. He would tell us if we drank it, he would be working in the hay soon and give us five dollars. He told us all kinds of lies. We believed him. I drank it and I got sick, of course. When Dad came home, I told him. He got onto him.

John, my oldest brother, was in the U.S. Navy. One day Mom saw him walking down the sidewalk to our house in town. He rode a bus from Springfield. Mom screamed and threw water all over the floor. When he got to our house she asked: "What do you want to eat?"

John said: "Toast."

So, all of us ate all the bread we had and wanted more. Mom sent me to the store. I got three more loaves of bread, and we ate all that too! Mom had churned cow cream for butter. It was so good. All six of us kids and Mom had butter on our faces. We were so happy my big brother was home from his tour of duty in Japan.

My brother John was beside our house on Walnut Street one day. He had a coconut.

I said: "What is it?"

He asked: "What is it? Well, it's a coconut." I asked: "Where did you get it?"

He said: "I found it up behind the grocery store."

So, my big mouth runs and tells Mom. I'm the mouth of the south.

She yelled: "John come here. Throw that away."

John said: "It's good. I charged it on Dad's bill. I just want to see how it tastes."

Mom made him crack it open and gave all of us kids a taste. I really didn't care for it.

CHAPTER 7

My Older Sister Janice

My sister Janice got a new can-can to make her full skirts stand way out. This was the style of the 1950s. Janice would starch it stiff to make it stand out better. Well, Naomi and I, my sister in crime, took the can-can and put it on our heads for a wedding vale. We marched up and down the path outside and hummed: "Dum dumda dum. Dum dumda dum."

We played with it so much that we ripped the lace. We secretly sewed it back but Janice saw our poor sewing job and found out. We got in big trouble. We never did play brides until we both wore real wedding dresses and veils on our wedding day.

CHAPTER 8

Mom Knew How to Give Us Whippings

When we got in trouble with Mom, she would tell us to get our own switch from the hedge. We had to get our own spanking for being bad. I was always setting her off. My mouth especially. She would switch me all up and down my legs. One day after my switching she made me lay down for my afternoon nap. I pinched the marks on my legs till Daddy came home from work. I showed him my legs.

Dad told Mom: "Don't be whipping my Horsey," the nickname he gave me.

I got the nickname when I was two years old. I was riding a pile of lumber, naked and yelling: "Hi Ho Silver," like the Lone Ranger on the radio. My uncle came up and took me into the house.

I thought after my spanking: *I'll show her. I'm going to get her in trouble.*

When Daddy took up for me Naomi said: "No Daddy. Glenda pinched her legs."

He and Mom thought it was funny. Not me.

Life went on and Mom said: "You little heifer. Go get a switch again."

So, I got a huge limb this time. I drug it inside.

Mom said: "What are you doing?"

I said: "Just go ahead and kill me." She got so tickled.

She said: "Take that outside and go ahead and play." She didn't get me after all.

18

CHAPTER 9

Sunday Drives
with Dad and Mom

On Sundays, Dad always liked to go out driving looking for some land to buy. He wanted out of town so badly where he could have animals and a big garden. We piled in the big back car seat, all four of us kids who were left at home. My brother and I always got into a fight every time. One Sunday Daddy stopped and put us both out of the car on a little side road. I was little and my brother wasn't very old either.

I asked Ronnie: "What are you going to do?"

He said: "I guess I will make us a tree house over there and we can be away from wild animals."

I felt better that he had a plan. But I never thought about any nails or anything to build with. Just in my little mind I thought: *Okay.*

All at once we heard: "Honk! Honk!" It was Daddy. We got in the car so fast. My mother told me for miles to stop my sniffling from crying. Once I started, I couldn't just stop. But my brother and I didn't fight anymore that day.

CHAPTER 10

We Made Believe Fun, Creative Things to Play

L ife was good with a big sister, me in the middle, and our baby sister Judy. We had fun playing with her. Just two houses down from ours lived a little boy named Davey. We would have pretend weddings for Judy and Davey with flowers in Judy's hair, an old dress of ours, and Mom's high heels—which I stole right out from under Mom's nose. I got so good at stealing that the older kids sent me after all kinds of things. They said I was good at it. I got to where I thought I could teach Naomi how to get things.

One day, we snuck into the kitchen and Naomi opened the refrigerator.

Mom said: "who is in that frigerator?" Naomi said: "It's me."

Mom yelled: "Get back outside."

I told Naomi outside: "You don't just open it up. You gently pull it open real slow."

She was supposed to get salt and butter. We were baking potatoes out of the garden in the trash can.

The bigger kids had me to do it all instead. They said: "You go Glenda."

I'd go right in and right out. We ate potatoes all afternoon. We washed them at the outside faucet and ate really good that day. Whatever they needed I always got it.

My older sister, Janice, got a new can-can that they called a slip to make your skirt stand out. Naomi and I got it one day and used it for a wedding veil outside.

We put it on our heads and hummed: "Dum dumda dum, dum dumda dum."

We threw wildflowers at our feet too. But we tore it along the bottom by stepping on it. We took it inside all dirty and ripped up. We got in trouble again. Mom sewed it up on her sewing machine. Janice washed and starched it, and it was good as new again.

Old Arthur Jack

Every day was an adventure. One day we went to see Arthur Jack. He lived behind us. His grand-kids lived in California. He always brought us a Dr. Pepper with cashews in it when we visited. It was so cold and so good on a hot summer day. We would sit on his porch. He would never let us go into his house. He told us all about California and his grandkids. He was a good old man. He would leave the pop bottles and let us keep them too.

After visiting Arthur Jack, we would go on down the road to Glenda and Fay's house. They were poor like us. We'd get the girls and take off up town. Arthur Jack gave me and Naomi a quarter. We always shared with our friends. Glenda Jones would go to the garage sometimes and get money from her dad who worked there. They always shared with us.

When our cousins came over, we usually went to the dump and got pop bottles. One Saturday we all went with the job of getting twenty-five cents each. The price of a movie ticket, small coke, and a bag of popcorn. We all were doing good and found five cents worth each. Then Sam, a mentally challenged boy, showed up. He yelled at us and told us he was going to get a gun and kill us all for getting his pop bottles. We got our bottles and left quickly. We ran home and told Daddy he was going to shoot us. Dad got up, walked up to Sam' house and told his dad what he said.

His dad laughed and said: "Ole Sam will not hurt you; he is a little off."

Daddy told him: "You keep him away from my girls and if you have a gun, you better hide it because I will go tell the Sheriff." Well, Ole Sam never threatened us again.

CHAPTER 12

Doling Park

On the 4th of July my cousins were always at our house. Mom cooked fried chicken. Made pies and bread and we would all go to Doling Park in Springfield for the fireworks. We'd ride the rides and go through the spook house and ride the merry-go- round. Dad gave us all fifty cents. We had to share with our cousins because their parents always just dropped them off so they could go honky tonkin' and drank way too much. They were terrible parents. So, we didn't mind sharing our little bit of money.

We would be down by the little river when we heard the first fireworks go off. That's when we ate supper on the park grounds and watched the fireworks. Judy had a big blanket on the ground. She would crawl all over the blanket but at the first "KABOOM" she was up on Daddy's lap. She would hide her face in Daddy's chest. After the fireworks stopped, we all piled in Daddy's car and went home. We were so tired. We ran all over looking at everything.

One 4th Mom got me and Naomi new sandals. I couldn't wear but one. I had stepped on a small coffee can that had its rim off and cut my foot. I had to wear a bandage. I was so upset. I wore a sock on my foot to cover my bandage. But I still rode a couple of rides. Doling Park was where my Aunt Mary Ellen and Uncle Pete met and they got married. They had four kids. I loved when Aunt Mary Ellen came over on Saturday night. She would bring popcorn and she would pop a dish pan full. Dad and Uncle Pete went to play pool. When we were too little to go the movies by ourselves, we watched Roy Rogers and Gunsmoke on TV and ate popcorn till we popped.

CHAPTER 13

Grandpa and Grandma's House

We would go to Grandma's house in Eureka Springs, Arkansas. She lived way up high above the stores. We would go downtown and play. Me, Naomi and Brenda, our other cousin. We walked on to the stores' roofs and went down their fire escape ladders to the street in front of the stores. We went all over that town. We would beg Uncle Richard for money and hew would give us a dollar. We thought we were rich. We stayed in town until almost dark and we knew we better get our butts home.

Coming up that hill we could smell Granny cooking fried chicken. Her food was better than any café. Our Grandpa was a grumpy old man. He told me every time I saw him the same stupid joke.

"You know why Arkansas girls don't wear ponytails? Cause they know what's under 'em."

I finally told him when I got older that Arkansas people don't use 911 because they can't find 11 on their phones. He did not laugh. He just spit tobacco in his nasty spit can. It felt good to see him not laugh or have an answer for my joke.

CHAPTER 14

The Apple Cider Explosion

One fall, Mom got a gallon jug of apple cider. She sat it under the sink. It was there and it was hot outside. Ronnie came in with his buddy Lynn. They drank a big glass of the apple cider and closed it up tight. They left and came back after a couple hours. My Dad was lighting the pilot light on our gas stove for the first time of the season to get it ready for winter. Just at that time, that jug of cider blowed up and made a loud "BANG!" Daddy rolled out the front door onto the porch. He thought the heating stove blowed up! Mom ran to the kitchen and saw that cider everywhere. Me and Naomi told Ronnie and Lynn what happened when they came running in from outside.

I asked: "Did you drink that cider because it was bad? It was no good and blew up."

They asked Mom: "Are we going to be alright?" Mom said: "It had soured."

Me and Naomi told them: "Don't jump around or move fast because you will blow up too."

They walked slowly, and Ronnie said: "I feel funny." So, they went outside to the outhouse. Our home-town of Republic had no sewer lines, and everyone had outhouses back then. Dad put lye in our outhouse a lot to keep the smell down. We laughed and laughed so hard because we finally got Ronnie back.

CHAPTER 15

The Mean, One-legged Rooster

My brother, Ronnie, brought home a one-legged baby chick one day. It grew up to be a one-legged, mean fighting rooster. Mom and Dad left for Springfield to get groceries and me and Naomi were left under Ronnie's care again. We were outside and here comes that mean rooster. Naomi ran and got into the house. I ran to the outhouse. That rooster stayed in front of that outhouse waiting for me to come out. I stayed in that stinky outhouse all day! Mom and Dad finally came home. Naomi ran and told Dad that Glenda has been in the outhouse all day. That rooster would not let her out. Dad came out there, grabbed that evil bird, and rung his neck. I finally came out all wet and sweating. It was so hot and stinky. I almost passed out.

We had fried chicken for dinner that night. My family was poor, and we didn't waste anything. I got the biggest piece I could get. I got my revenge.

CHAPTER 16

Politics and Pepto Bismol

Halloween time came so Naomi and I went and got our share of candy. We also gave out "Nixon for President" campaign leaflets. We heard Kennedy was Catholic and we would have to eat fish every Friday. At school, we had fish every Friday anyway because we had a few Catholic kids. Well, you know what choice we made. Now, I love fish so much I could eat fish every day.

We were good kids, but we were into a lot of mischief. One time, Naomi swallowed a nickel. She got to eat bananas. I was jealous. I tried swallowing a nickel too but couldn't. Another time, Mom put me on a white slip. She said it looked like a little sundress. The neighbor kids laughed and laughed at me. They could tell it wasn't a dress. So, Naomi sprayed water on me from the outside faucet. I went in like I was crying and told Mom that Ronnie did it. She changed me into a real dress then. Mom jumped onto Ronnie, and he didn't know what in the world she was talking about.

There was an old, half-crazy man named Oliver who lived above the laundry in town. We liked doing laundry and seeing Oliver. One day we accidently put bleach on Daddy's new jeans. He was so mad he told Mom to go up there and do the laundry.

But Oliver told us: "Go home. Go home now and do the dishes."

We would tell him: "No. You go home."

Every time we would see him uptown, he'd say: "Go home. Do the dishes."

We were afraid of him. He wore the same clothes all the time and an old brown hat that was all worn out. We thought he looked like a bum and a clown.

One night after supper, Dad was eating cornbread and milk. He loved it so much. He got choked badly and even fell in the floor. The boys were laughing at him. I didn't know what was wrong with him. He finally got it down and got up.

He yelled: "You crazy boys, let a man die just to get a laugh!" Then he said a few words that I cannot repeat. He was sure mad.

That summer, my mom took care of my cousin Paul for extra money. She had us to go out and play. He lived two blocks behind us. Naomi didn't want to play so we went outside to ask Paul to go get something good to drink. He came out with a half bottle of Pepto Bismol.

I told him: "It smells like liquid bubble gum." We shared it. He liked it and I loved it!

Paul said: "We have a big bottle at home." I said: "Go get it, Paul."

While he was gone, I made noise and talked so Mom didn't miss him. He went fast and came back with a large bottle, not even opened. We opened it easily because there was no child proof lock on medicine in the 1950s. We drank it and began feeling not so good.

I said: "Let's go sit on the porch."

I looked at Paul. He had a good tan, but his face was kind of green and around his lips was a thin, blue line.

I asked him: "How do I look?"

He said: "Really white with a blue ring around your lips." About then we both ran to the back yard by the outhouse and threw up a lot of pink stuff. We were like the commercial:

"Upset tummy, indigestion, and diarrhea," only we were like this for days. It didn't work like the commercial said. To this day, at age 75, I sure can't take a spoon full. It's funny how you get so sick on something that smelled like liquid bubble gum.

CHAPTER 17

Chickens for Sale

A t the end of that summer, me and Naomi came up with the idea to kill two chickens. We were little but we had watched Mom so many times. We just knew we could do it. We tried to hang them on the clothesline. It didn't work because their necks stretched until their heads were on the ground.

Finally, I said: "We got to kill them."

I got an axe and did it like I seen Daddy do it. We put them in hot water and took their feathers off. We cut them open and closed our eyes. We each pulled out the guts.

Ronnie and Lynn came and asked: "What are you doing?" He told us how much trouble we were in.

When we said: "We're selling them to Mrs. Whipple," he changed his tone.

So, we took two big hens and got five dollars. We came home. Ronnie and Lynn were waiting to ask how much we got.

We were excited and told him: "Five dollars!"

Ronnie said: "Well me and Lynn are working next week. If you give us the money, we will give you ten dollars. Five each." So, me and Naomi agreed. *We are both old ladies now and we have never got our five dollars!* Ronnie and Lynn took off to the pool hall.

The next week was "Dooms Day." Mrs. Whipple called mom and wanted two more of them big, baking hens to put into her freezer.

Mom asked her: "Who sold you two chickens?" Mrs. Whipple said: "Your little girls."

Mom went to the hen house. It was two of her setting hens! She was so mad. The eggs were no good, so she trashed them. And boy did we get it with a switch.

She yelled: "I am going to make you two dance from my switching!"

And we sure did! Ronnie got in trouble from Dad for taking our money. Life sure wasn't dull.

CHAPTER 18

Old Aunt Mattie and Uncle Jess

Winter finally comes and Aunt Mattie moved in after Dad's brother died. She gave me a long flannel gown. She put Vick's vapor rub all over me and put that gown on me. She picked me to sleep with her.

She told me every night, "Now, if I die in the night—when you get up, first go tell your Daddy."

I was so scared that I couldn't sleep.

So, after a month, I told Daddy: "I just can't sleep at all with her."

I told him what she said. So, he told me to go sleep with my sisters. I was so glad she took my gown back.

When we were little, sometimes I wouldn't eat what was for supper. I would go tell Daddy I was hungry. He always got up and fried me two eggs. Then I was fine. I started school and Mom was going with my Aunt Hazel for peaches. I didn't know why but she fixed our lunches. That day, my first day of school, I asked Naomi everything about school.

She said: "When the bell rings eat your lunch."

A bell rang later. I thought *why are the kids all leaving*? So, I ate my lunch. The kids came back in and another bell rings.

The teacher said: "Everyone. It's lunch time." I didn't know what to do so I asked Naomi.

She said: "All I have is a powdered doughnut." I said: "I hate them. I have one too."

So, I thought *I am going to die*! I went home. Mom wasn't there. I began to cry. So, I thought *I will go to Uncle Jess Alley's house*. I told him I was going to die because I ate my lunch too early.

He laughed and said: "I have beef noodles. You can eat some and I will take you back to school."

I ate a big bowl full. He took me back to school. Naomi was waiting. She was afraid because I was never alone. She didn't know where I went. I finally learned all the bells and went to school.

CHAPTER 19

A Move to the Farm

When we were older, we moved to the country onto a farm on Highway 174. When school was out and after our chores were done there wasn't much to do on the farm. This was now in the 1960s and Interstate 44 wasn't even built or thought of.

My oldest sister Janice and Mom were sitting in the shade under a big, old oak tree. We didn't have air conditioning and it was hot. Janice was big and pregnant. All the eighteen wheelers came down Highway 174 back then. I snuck behind my sister and Mom motioning for each truck to honk its horn. I was pulling down the hammer.

Every truck would honk very long blasts for me. Mom and Janice got so mad. They thought the truckers were flirting with them. I was behind them rolling with laughter. I think I heard my Mom even say a few cuss words. I heard Janice ask:

"Can't they see I am pregnant?"

When they finally caught me, I got into a bit of trouble. Daddy thought it was hilarious.

CHAPTER 20

The Country Church

Living in the country on the farm caused us to lose our little gang of friends. We started to church way out on 39 Highway. We were now teenagers. The boys were after me and Naomi. We wrote their names on our bedroom wall and hearts all over. That's when we had a church gang: Joyce Kay, my sister-in- law Hazel's sister. Hazel is John' wife, my older brother. We had Janice Norris, Brenda her cousin, and Brosha her sister.

At church, the boys, a lot of them, stayed outside. The windows had screens on them and were open because it was summertime. The boys blew cigarette smoke in the church. My Dad thought that was so funny, but the preacher's husband didn't think it was. The lady preacher had little kids. I would change the baby boy's diapers. I had practice babysitting. I had stayed a month in St. Louis with my sister Janice. Her baby boy, Todd, I got to spoil.

At church, Denny Wolf played a guitar. He asked to take me home one time. He kissed me. I hated it. He kissed me like a plunger over my mouth. My whole face was wet! I thought *how can I get rid of him?* A lady preacher came for revival. Her little fat daughter, Glenda, had the hots for the "Wolf Man." Her mother told him God told her He was with the wrong Glenda. Her Glenda was the chosen one. He told me in the car he had to go with the other Glenda because God had said. I was so happy.

I said: "Hallelujah!"

He said: "But I want a kiss goodbye?"

I said: "No Denny, you need to save them kisses for Glenda D."

40

I won't say her name, but Glenda D. got the sloppiest, nasty kisser around.

I told Joyce Kay and Naomi I was going to dump him. They said: "No, he is cute and plays guitar."

I said: "I set him up for you all." But they said: "No, we don't want plunger lips."

This little guy Howard started following me around. He would sing the song "I Saw Glenda Yesterday," a very popular song back then. I probably wouldn't have dated him if he didn't sing that song. My heart went up and down like a roller coaster, and round and round like a merry go round because of that song.

Janice always wore bright red lipstick and her boyfriend Cecil always had lip marks on his face. I always thought for sure they would get married.

CHAPTER 21

A New Life and Marriage

But after revival we went to a church in Springfield at a store front. We met Lois and Sammy Cook and their daughter Evelyn. She worked every day but Sammy, not so much. Daddy always said Sam was a "go get-her." Lois would get off work and he would go get her. We met the Johnson brothers. Naomi met Earl and I met Charles. Charles and I got married young.

Charles got drafted for Vietnam, so Mom and Dad said: "You better marry that boy. He might get killed over there." I was in the 10th grade, almost in the 11th grade.

I said: "I ain't getting married till I got to graduate." My parents wanted me to marry him before he had to go to Nam. I did finish high school years later.

In 1972, Charles got killed by a drunk driver. But this is all for the next book. A lot happened to two little broke girls. We both made it to adult hood. Our good life, our fun sunny days were behind us. We were poor but we had love.

We are out in the big world now still trying to make it with Jesus leading us both. All the years gone by and we're old now and have been through a lot; but we're still here.

The End

Printed in the United States
by Baker & Taylor Publisher Services